QUANTUM
QUANDARIES

QUANTUM QUANDARIES

100 BRAINTEASERS FROM

THE MAGAZINE OF MATH AND SCIENCE

Edited by
TIMOTHY WEBER

Illustrated by
SERGEY IVANOV

Introduction by
MARK SAUL, Ph.D.

ISBN 0-87355-136-2

NSTA Stock #PB123X

Printed in the U.S.A. by Automated Graphics

As the language of science, mathematics is universal. And yet it has its dialects. Counting on their fingers, Europeans start with the thumb, while Americans start with the index finger, saving the thumb for number five. The notation for an angle in English is not quite the same as that used in French. The binomial coefficients have nine or ten symbols worldwide, some of which mean different things in different cultures.

Do all these surface differences reflect deeper differences in thought or content? It's not clear. What *is* clear is that even mathematics—that purest form of human thought—has a cultural element. The development of mathematics at different times and in different places is linked, in some mysterious way, to other elements of *culture*—the form of adaptation to the environment that is so characteristic of our species. We are not in control of the fonts of our creativity. So it is important that we stay open to a variety of influences: who knows where we will get our next insight?

This book contains the first 100 "brainteasers" from *Quantum: The Magazine of Math and Science.* They are the product of one of the most mathematically creative cultures of our century—most of them first appeared in the Russian journal *Kvant* over the past 25 years. (The poetic Russian word for them—*golovolomki*—means, literally, "head breakers"!) My colleagues in Moscow, Vladimir Dubrovsky, Alexander Buzdin, and Albert Stasenko (*Quantum* field editors), have selected brainteasers that range from light fare—almost jokes or riddles—to serious problem situations that can be pursued ever deeper. Some will be familiar to the reader (this is inevitable), while others will be fresh. None requires a lot of mathematical background, at least for an initial approach. And many are quotable, having already entered the mathematical "folklore" in which some of the best problems are enshrined. In the pages that follow, the author of the brainteaser (if known) is indicated in parentheses at the end of the solution.

In selecting material for *Quantum*, we generally filter out the most idiosyncratically Russian brainteasers that have appeared in our sister magazine *Kvant*. Some of these involve details of Russian life (like the tetrahedral cartons used to package milk or the preparation of "a nice breakfast *kasha*") that our readers might find confusing. But some of the brainteasers in *Quantum* and in this book spring from the colorful pages of Russian fairy tales, giving them an exotic air. In every case, though, the mathematics survives the translation, and some of the Russian flavor still clings.

Although I have been talking exclusively about mathematics, you will find some brainteasers here that challenge you to think about ordinary physical processes and strange phenomena (real and hypothetical). *Quantum*'s field editor for physics, Larry D. Kirkpatrick, Ph.D., had a hand in polishing these problems. I might be forgiven for stressing the mathematics—not only is it my profession, but physics is virtually "mathematics in action" in the real world. The name of our magazine gives the game away: the basic thrust of *Quantum* is quantification—not merely tallying or categorizing, but finding the math that *explains*.

We hope you enjoy working on these brainteasers and can see them as a small part the rich tradition of Russian mathematics. Perhaps you will begin to examine other mathematical traditions. Maybe you will view your own with new eyes. The mix of mathematics and culture offers much to ponder.

—Mark Saul, Ph.D.
Quantum Field Editor for Mathematics

Acknowledgments

Special thanks to Elisabeth Tobia, for her skillful management of the publication process; to Ken Roberts, for coming up with our alliterative title; and to all those who have contributed brainteasers to *Kvant* and *Quantum* magazine over the years.

Irregular but predictable

It's easy to show that the sum of the five acute angles of a regular star (like the ones in the American flag or the one in the Soviet flag) is 180°. Prove that the sum of the five angles of an irregular star is also 180°.

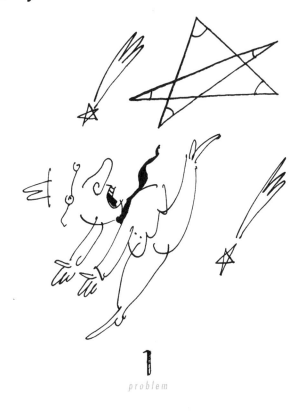

Irregular but predictable

Join two of the star's adjacent vertices—say, A and E. Since the angles at M of triangles AME and BMD are congruent, the sum of the angles B and D of triangle BMD equals the sum of the angles A and E of triangle AME; but then the total sum of angles at the vertices of the star is equal to the sum of the angles of triangle ACE—that is, 180°. (A. Korshkov)

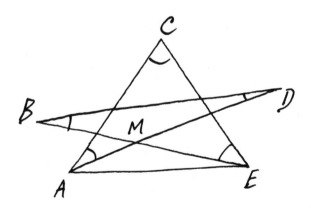

Expanding gap

Using each of the numbers 1, 2, 3, and 4 twice, I succeeded in writing out an eight-digit number in which there is one digit between the ones, two digits between the twos, three digits between the threes, and four digits between the fours. What was the number?

Expanding gap

There are two such numbers: 41312432 and 23421314. (A. Savin)

Big difference

Write the numbers 1 to 8 in the eight circles shown so that any two numbers inside circles joined by a line differ by no less than 2.

Big difference

The solution is shown below. You first determine that the numbers 1 and 8 must be put in the middle (since they are each joined to six other circles); then the position of the numbers 2 and 7 can be uniquely determined; then the number 3 and the others can be placed. (Obviously, the solution can be flipped along its vertical axis, in which case the outer pairs 3-5 and 4-6 would swap positions.) (A. Domashenko)

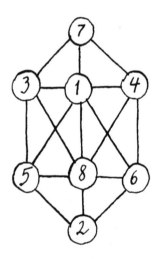

4

Fast and slow

My grandfather's clock behaves in a strange way. During the first half hour of every hour it's two minutes fast, but during the second half hour it's two minutes slow. How can that be explained?

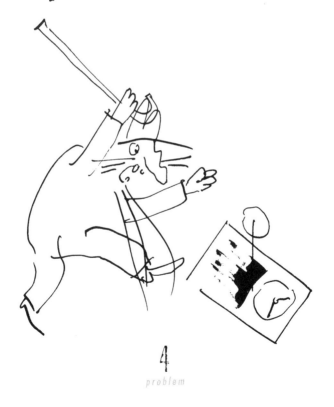

4

Fast and slow

The clock keeps time correctly, but the minute hand is slightly loose on its spindle—it can move freely two minutes from its correct position. Under the action of the force of gravity, the minute hand always stays below its correct position. In the left half of the clock dial, this makes the clock two minutes slow; in the right half, two minutes fast. (A. Panov)

Equilateral equality

An arbitrary point inside an equilateral triangle is joined to the three vertices and perpendicular lines are dropped down to the three sides. Show that the sum of the areas of the three gray triangles equals that of the three white ones.

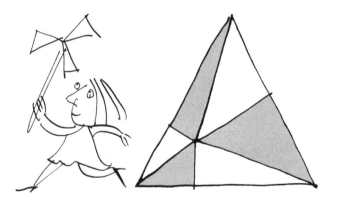

Equilateral equality

If lines parallel to the sides of the triangle are drawn through the chosen point, pairs of congruent triangles of different colors are formed. (B. Proizvolov)

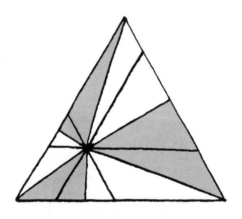

Safe transit

How can a goat, a head of cabbage, two wolves, and a dog be transported across a river if it's known that the wolf is "culinarily partial to" goat and dog, the dog is "on bad terms with" the goat, and the goat is "not indifferent to" cabbage? There are only three seats in your boat, so you can take only two passengers—animal or vegetable—at a time.

Safe transit

Keeping the goat in the boat, take the dog and then the cabbage across the river. Take the goat back and leave it on the riverbank (all by itself). Take the two wolves across the river. Return with the dog. In the last crossing take the dog and the goat across. (E. Chernyshov)

A mean shot

Thirty people took part in a shooting match. The first participant scored 80 points, the second scored 60 points, the third scored the arithmetic mean of the number of points scored by the first two, and each subsequent competitor scored the arithmetic mean of the number of points scored by all the previous ones. How many points did the last competitor score?

solution

A mean shot

The answer is 70. This problem is based on the fact that adding the mean value of a set of numbers to this set gives a set with the same mean value. (N. Antonovich)

solution

Totally odd

When we multiply multidigit numbers, we have to do some addition as well—the final step is to sum the subtotals. Here's a puzzle that exposes the steps and tags the various digits as odd ("O") or even ("E"):

$$
\begin{array}{r}
\times\ E\ E\ O \\
O\ O \\
\hline
+\ E\ O\ E\ O \\
E\ O\ O \\
\hline
O\ O\ O\ O\ O
\end{array}
$$

even?… Odd!

Find numbers that satisfy this scheme.

Totally odd

See the figure below. (A. Savin)

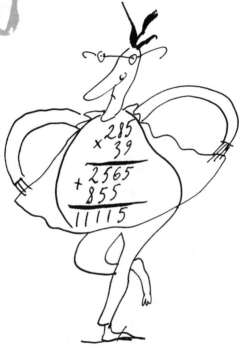

Subsurface tension

A scuba diver loses his bearings deep in the ocean. How can he tell which way to go to get to the surface?

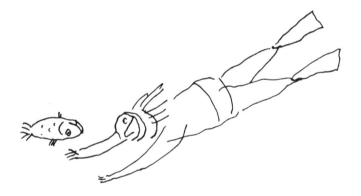

Subsurface tension

The diver can tell which way is up by watching the bubbles coming out of his breathing apparatus or by dropping a pebble. (B. Proizvolov)

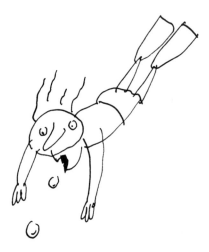

10

Power failure

Will a candle burn in a spaceship, where everything is weightless?

solution 10

Power failure

Combustion occurs when there is an influx of oxygen. Under ordinary conditions on Earth the influx of oxygen is due to convection: near the flame heated air, which is lighter, ascends together with the products of combustion; colder air, containing oxygen, takes their place. In the state of weightlessness there will be no convection, and the flame will die from a lack of oxygen. (I. Slobodetsky, L. Aslamazov)

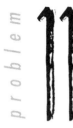

Drawing the line

How can a polygonal line *BDEFG* be drawn in a triangle *ABC* so that the five triangles obtained have the same area?

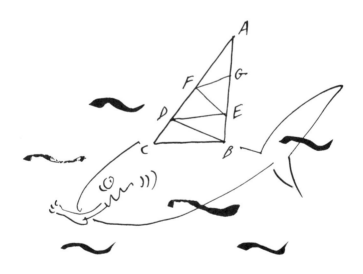

Drawing the line

Point *D* should be positioned so that segment *CD* is equal to 1/5 of segment *AC*; then the area of triangle *DBC* will be 1/5 that of *ABC*. Similarly, point *E* is positioned so that *BE* = *AB*/4, point *F* so that *FD* = *AD*/3, and point *G* so that *EG* = *AE*/2. (A. Savin)

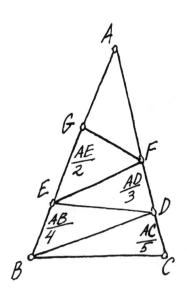

Billions and billions

The product of a billion natural numbers is equal to a billion. What's the greatest value the sum of these numbers can have?

Billions and billions

Answer: 1,999,999,999. If there are two numbers a and b greater than 1 among the given numbers, then, replacing one of them with ab and the other with 1, we'll retain the product of all the numbers and increase their sum, because the inequality $(a - 1)/(b - 1) > 0$ implies that $ab + 1 > a + b$. Thus, the sum will be greatest if one of the numbers is a billion and all the others are equal to 1. (G. Galperin)

Optimist vs. pessimist

A glass flask of an irregular shape contains a certain amount of liquid. Is it possible to tell (without any measuring devices or other containers) whether the flask is more or less than half full?

13

Optimist vs. pessimist

Mark the level of the liquid and turn the
flask upside down. (M. Lobak)

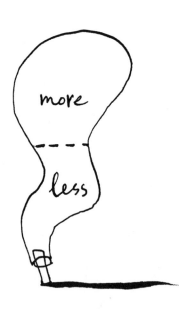

more

less

Foursquare integrity

Is it possible to add four digits to the right of the number 9999 so that the eight-digit number obtained becomes the square of an integer?

Foursquare integrity

No, since every such number is less than $10{,}000^2$ but greater than $9{,}999^2 = 99{,}980{,}001$. (Y. Kurlyandchik)

In their own worlds

Winnie-the-Pooh and Piglet went to visit each other. They started at the same time and walked along the same road. But since Winnie-the-Pooh was absorbed in composing a new "hum" and Piglet was trying to count up all the birds overhead, they didn't notice one another when they met. A minute after the meeting Winnie-the-Pooh was at Piglet's, and four minutes after the meeting Piglet was at Winnie-the-Pooh's. How long had each of them walked?

In their own worlds

Winnie-the-Pooh had walked for 3 minutes and Piglet for 6 minutes. Suppose it took x minutes for Winnie-the-Pooh and Piglet to walk from their respective homes W and P to the meeting point M. Winnie-the-Pooh spent x minutes walking from W to M and 1 minute from M to P; therefore, $WM/MP = x$. The same reasoning for Piglet gives $PM/MW = x/4$. Since $WM/MP \cdot PM/MW = 1$, $x^2/4 = 1$, which gives us $x = 2$. (S. Sefibekov)

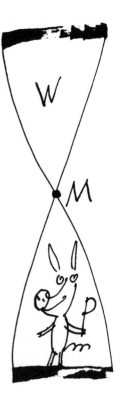

Simple question

Is this pattern symmetrical?

Simple question

No, it isn't symmetrical. Notice that turning one of the stars upside down gives us a figure with central symmetry. (G Galperin)

Color balance

problem

You have two red balls, two blue ones, two green, two yellow, and two white. A number of balls of different colors are placed on the left pan of a balance, while the other balls of the same colors are put on the right one. The balance tips to the left. If you exchange any pair of balls of the same color, however, the balance either tips to the right or stays even. How many balls are there on the balance?

Color balance

First, notice that each ball on the left pan is heavier than the ball of the same color on the right (otherwise there's a ball on the left that's lighter than the ball of the same color on the right, and we can then exchange them without tipping the balance). If there are no less than three balls on each side, we could exchange the pair of balls with minimum mass differences without affecting the balance. So there are at most two balls on each side. Obviously, there can be one ball in each pan. Two balls are also possible provided that the mass difference for each pair of balls of the same color is the same. (V. Proizvolov)

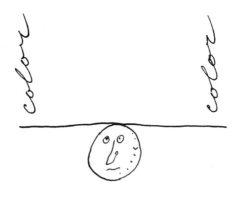

18

Matchmaking

Move a single match in each row to get a true equality.

$$V = II + VIII$$

$$VI = II + VIII$$

$$VII = II + VIII$$

Matchmaking

See the figure below (the last line should be read as "7 = |1 − 8|"). (N. Rodina)

$$X = II + VIII$$

$$-VI = II - VIII$$

$$VII = II - VIII I$$

Cuts and corners

A square is cut into a number of rectangles in such a way that no point of the square is a common vertex of four rectangles. Prove that the number of points of the square that are the vertices of rectangles is even.

Cuts and corners

Four vertices are at the corners of the square. Each of the vertices inside the square is a common vertex of exactly two rectangles. Let n be the number of rectangles into which the square is cut, m the number of points of the square that are common vertices of exactly two rectangles. The total number of vertices for all the rectangles can now be calculated in two ways. On one side it's equal to $4n$; on the other it's equal to $4 + 2m$. So $m = 2(n - 1)$, which is an even number. Adding the four corners of the square we get $m + 4$, which is also even. (L. Salakhov)

Quicksilver question

A steel ball floats in mercury. Will the depth of immersion increase or decrease as the temperature rises?

Quicksilver question

The thermal expansion of mercury is greater than that of steel, so the force pushing the ball upward decreases and the ball sinks lower. (L. Steingraz)

21

Singular product

Bobby added together three consecutive integers, then the next three numbers, and multiplied one sum by the other. Could the product be equal to 111,111,111?

Singular product

No, it can't. One of the two triples of numbers must contain an even number and two odd ones. Their sum is even, so the product of the two sums must be even. (S. Genkin)

two odd ones

Playing with matches

A spiral made of 35 matchsticks is wound clockwise. Shift four matches to rewind it counterclockwise.

Playing with matches

See the figure below. (A. Domashenko)

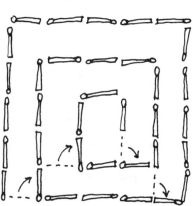

Clever removal

You can do either of two things to a number written on the blackboard: you can double it, or you can erase the last digit. How can you get 14 starting from 458 by using these two operations?

Clever removal

If we denote by *D* and *E* the operations of doubling and erasing, then one of the possible sequences of operations is *D, E, E, D, D, D, E, D*, resulting in the sequence of numbers 458, 916, 91, 9, 18, 36, 72, 7, 14. (D. Fomin)

Half-stop

Two parallel diagonals are drawn in a regular octagon. Prove that the area of the rectangle obtained is half the area of the entire octagon.

Half-stop

See the figure below, in which equal figures have the same shading. (V. Proizvolov)

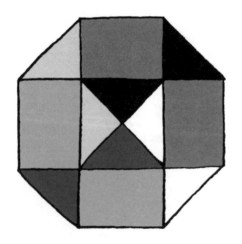

25

Burning question

The smoke we see consists of small particles of unburned fuel. Each of the particles is much heavier than air. So why do they fly upward?

Burning question

Unburned particles (smoke) are lifted by an upward flow of hot air. When the surrounding air cools, the particles begin to drop and eventually settle to the ground.

Mix and match

There are three red and five blue sticks of different lengths lying on the table. The total length of the red sticks is the same as that of the blue ones. Is it possible to cut up the sticks and pair the pieces such that the pieces in each pair will be alike in length but different in color?

Mix and match

Yes. Place the sticks so as to make two parallel rows, red and blue, one below the other, and cut each row right at the gaps between sticks in the other row. (V. Proizvolov)

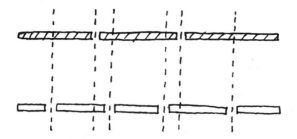

Comparing ages

Now I'm four times older than my sister was when she was half as young as I was. In 15 years our combined age will be 100. How old are we now?

Comparing ages

I'm 40 and my sister is 30. If my sister was n years old when she was half as old as I was, I was then $2n$ and am now $4n$ years old. So now she is $n + (4n - 2n) = 3n$, and in 15 years we'll be $4n + 15$ and $3n + 15$. The equation $(4n + 15) + (3n + 15) = 100$ yields $n = 10$.

I am n years old, brother

Go with the flow

Once I got lost in a forest. I was going to make a fire and spend the night, but fortunately I found a water pipe. Obviously I should go along the pipe, but in what direction? In the direction of the water flow, since the water goes to people. But how could I determine in which direction the water was flowing?

Go with the flow

I made a fire under the pipe, walked a little ways along the pipe in both directions, and put my hand on it to find out where the pipe was warmer. The water was flowing in this direction. (M. Lobak)

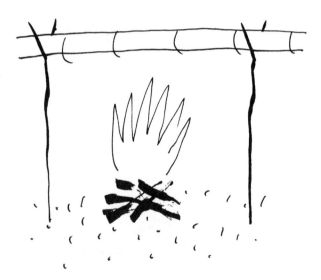

The algebra of cooperation

Solve the number rebus

USA + USSR = PEACE.

(The same letters stand for the same digits, different letters denote different digits.)

The algebra of cooperation

$932 + 9{,}338 = 10{,}270$. Clearly the sum is greater than 10,000 but less than 11,000, so P = 1, E = 0, U = 9. Then A + R = 10, $1 + S + S = C$ (if $1 + 2 \cdot S = C + 10$, then in the next decimal place we'd have S = A), and $9 + S = A + 10$. Finally, we get the system of equations A + R = 10, $2 \cdot S + 1 = C$, S = A + 1. The letter C denotes an odd number ($2 \cdot S + 1$), which is less than 9 (9 has already been assigned to U). On the other hand, $C = 2 \cdot S + 1 = 2 \cdot A + 3 \geq 2 \cdot 2 + 3 = 7$, since A ≥ 2 (1 has already been assigned to P). Thus, C = 7. All that remains is to calculate the other digits and check the answer. (B. Kruglikov)

The wisdom of old

King Arthur ordered a pattern for his quarter-circle shield. He wanted it to be painted in three colors: yellow, the color of kindness; red, the color of courage: and blue, the color of wisdom. When the artist brought in his work, the king's armor-bearer said there was more courage than wisdom on the shield. But the artist managed to prove that the proportions of both virtues were equal. Can you tell how?

The wisdom of old

Sector *ABC* is 1/8 of the circle with radius *AB*; semicircle *AB* is 1/2 of the circle with radius *AB*/2. So these two figures are equal in area. Subtracting the shaded area *ABD* from both of them, we get the required equality. (A.Savin)

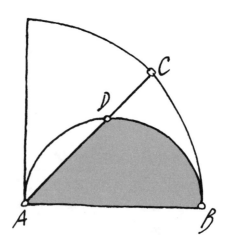

Summed divisor

Prove that at least one of any 18 successive three-digit numbers is divisible by the sum of its digits.

Summed divisor

One of any 18 successive numbers is divisible by 18; so the sum S of its digits is divisible by 9, and the last digit is even. Since the number has 3 digits, S is not greater than $9 + 9 + 8 = 26$; so $S = 9$ or $S = 18$. In both cases S divides into the chosen number. (S. Yeliseyev)

Study in black and gray

Which part of the square has the greater area: the black part or the gray part?

RUSSIAN ART

Study in black and gray

Adding the dark-gray areas to the area of the black part of the square, we get the area of triangle *BCF*, which is half that of the whole square. Similarly, the sum of the same dark-gray areas and the light-gray areas is equal to the area of the square minus the area of triangle *ABE*, which is also half the area of the square. So the black part and the light-gray part are equal. (V. Proizvolov)

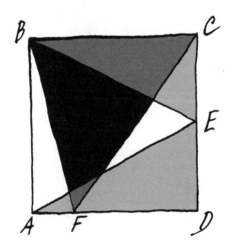

Mercurial clock

In some antique clocks intended for operation in the open air, the pendulum was a long tube with a container of mercury at the bottom. What was the purpose of this design?

Mercurial clock

As the temperature increases, the pendulum's length also increases, but the mercury, because its volume increases, goes up the tube. A proper selection of the volume of mercury and the diameter of the tube makes it possible to keep the distance from the pendulum's point of suspension to its center of gravity constant. As a result of this design the pendulum's period of oscillation doesn't depend on temperature and the clock's accuracy is increased. (A. Buzdin)

Startling star

Write the numbers 1 to 11 in the circles so that the sum of the four numbers at the vertices of each of the five sectors of the star equals 25.

Startling star

See the figure below. (N. Avilov)

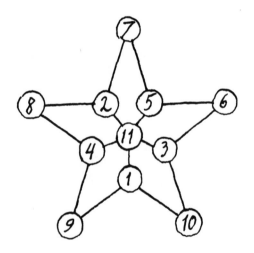

Boxed in

Is it possible to wrap a cube in the stairlike piece of paper shown below so that its entire surface is covered without overlaps?

Boxed in

See the figure below. Two opposite faces of the cube are covered with four small triangles each; a third face is covered with the two bigger triangles; the three other faces are covered with the square portions of the given sheet. (N. Dolbilin)

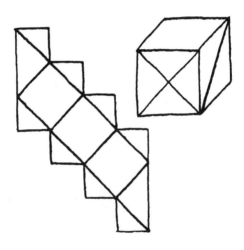

Restore the product

The figure shows a product in which some of the figures are rubbed out and replaced by asterisks. Restore the absent figures.

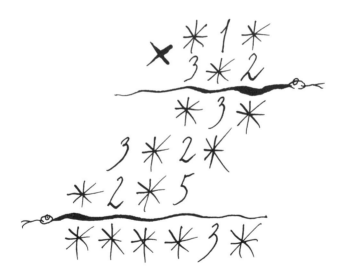

Restore the product

See the figure below. (L. Yakovleva)

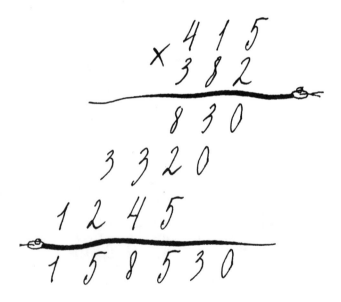

$$
\begin{array}{r}
4\ 1\ 5 \\
\times\ 3\ 8\ 2 \\
\hline
8\ 3\ 0 \\
3\ 3\ 2\ 0 \\
1\ 2\ 4\ 5 \\
\hline
1\ 5\ 8\ 5\ 3\ 0
\end{array}
$$

37

Jug, pot, and barrel

You have a four-liter jug, a six-liter pot, and a big barrel of water. Can you measure exactly one liter of water?

Jug, pot, and barrel

Fill the pot and tilt it as shown below. Because of the symmetry of the cylinder, 3 liters of water will be left. Now fill the jug and pour 3 liters into the pot (until the pot is full). Then exactly 1 liter of water will be left in the jug. (G. Kushnirenko)

3 liters

Possibility of trisection

One of the three famous ancient geometrical problems is the problem of trisecting an angle with ruler and compass. It was proved long ago that this problem, along with the other two, is in general unsolvable. But there are some exceptions to this rule. Trisect an angle of 54° using only a compass (that is, construct points that lie on the rays dividing the angle into three congruent parts).

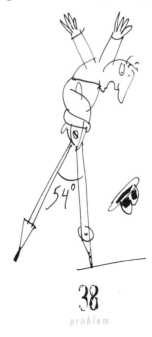

Possibility of trisection

Draw a circle whose center is at the vertex O of the given angle; label the points where it meets the arms of the angle A and B. Using only a compass we can successively mark points C, D, E, and F on the circle such that $AC = AO$, $BD = BC$, $DE = DC$, and $EF = EB$. Then points E and F lie on the trisectors of the angle, since $\angle BOC = \angle DOB = 60° - 54° = 6°$, $\angle BOE = \angle EOF = 18° = 54°/3$. (A. Shvetsov)

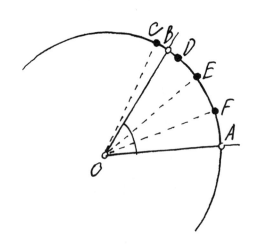

39

Turning seven by fives

Seven coins lie along a circle. Can you turn them all upside down if you're only allowed to turn over any five coins in succession at a time? Can you do it by turning over a succession of four coins at a time?

Turning seven by fives

Label the coins 1, 2, 3, 4, 5, 6, 7 in clockwise order. Turn over coins 1, 2, 3, 4, 5, then 2, 3, 4, 5, 6, and so on seven times, each time shifting the first coin of the succession one position clockwise, so that the last group is 7, 1, 2, 3, 4. Each time we turn over five coins, so every coin will be turned over five times and eventually will stay upside down.

Turning four coins over at a time, one can't turn all seven of them over. To see this, write +1 on the heads of the coins and −1 on the tails. Then turning a coin over amounts to changing the sign on its upper side. When we turn four coins over, four signs are changed, so the product of all +1's and −1's on the upper sides of the coins always stays the same, whereas after turning over all seven coins it would have changed its sign.

Try to prove that with the "fivefold moves" one can turn over any given subset of the seven coins, and with the "fourfold moves" any subset having an even number of coins. (A. Shvetsov)

Traveling light

Dashing sea captains wouldn't fill their holds completely when they transported cotton from Australia to England. It would have been to their advantage to take as much as they could, but they didn't. Why not?

40

Traveling light

While being transported overseas, cotton absorbs moisture and so gets heavier. The captains made allowance for this increase in the cotton's weight. (L. Mochalov)

Mystery of the stars

The moons in the accompanying number rebus denote one and the same digit. This scanty information is enough to uniquely restore all the figures represented by the stars, which denote different digits. Try to do it.

s o l u t i o n

Mystery of the stars

The answer is shown below. It follows from the very form of the product that the second digit of the second factor is zero. The product has the form $1111m = 271 \cdot 41m$, where m is the digit denoted by the Moon. The numbers 271 and 41 are prime, so the first factor in the given sum is 271; to find the second we must choose m so that $41m$ is a three-digit number whose second digit is zero. The only suitable m is 5; then $41m = 205$. (V. Denisenko).

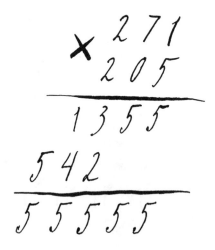

$$\begin{array}{r} 2\,7\,1 \\ \times\ 2\,0\,5 \\ \hline 1\,3\,5\,5 \\ 5\,4\,2 \\ \hline 5\,5\,5\,5\,5 \end{array}$$

Look through the telescope

A fly has gotten onto the lens of a telescope. What will an observer looking through the telescope see?

Look through the telescope

Practically nothing will change: the fly won't be seen. But if it covers a rather large portion of the lens, remote objects will appear to be slightly less bright. (V. Surdin)

Enlightening eclipse

A girl watched a solar eclipse with her father.

"Daddy, how much further away from us is the Sun than the Moon?"

"As far as I remember, 387 times further."

"Then I can figure out how much greater the Sun is in volume than the Moon."

Her father thought a bit and said, "I think maybe you can."

So what is the ratio of the volumes of the two heavenly bodies?

Enlightening eclipse

During an eclipse the Moon covers the Sun almost completely. So the Sun's radius is to the Moon's radius as the Sun's distance from the Earth is to the Moon's distance from the Earth—that is, 387:1. So the ratio of the volumes of the Sun and Moon is approximately $387^3 : 1$. (A. Kozlov)

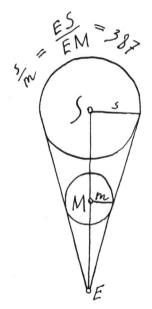

$$\frac{S}{m} = \frac{ES}{EM} = 387$$

Writing home

Can astronauts use a ballpoint pen on board a spacecraft? What about a fountain pen? What design would you recommend for a "space pen"?

solution 44

Writing home

A ballpoint pen can't be used in the state of weightlessness because the thick ink is pressed against the ball under the action of gravity. (If you've ever tried to write against a wall or with the tip of the pen pointed upward, you will have verified this fact.) The operation of a fountain pen, on the other hand, is based on capillary action. So a fountain pen will work in a state of weightlessness. (A. Buzdin)

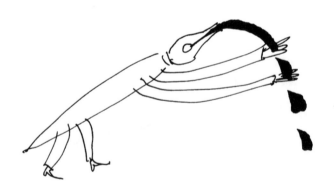

Fashion statement

Three girls went out in white, green, and blue dresses. Their shoes were also one of these three colors. (Each wore a matched pair of shoes!) Only Anna had the same color dress as shoes. Neither Betty's dress nor her shoes were white, and Katie's shoes were green. What was the color of each girl's dress?

Fashion statement

Since Katie's shoes were green, her dress was not. And since Katie's shoes were green, Anna's shoes were not, and therefore her dress was not. So the green dress must belong to Betty.

What color are her shoes? They cannot be white, and they cannot be green. So Betty's shoes must be blue. Then Anna is wearing the white shoes and therefore also the white dress. The blue dress is left for Katie.

Water fractions

A barrel was full of water. All the water was poured in equal portions into three pails. It turned out that the water took up 1/2 of the volume of the first pail, 2/3 of the volume of the second pail, and 3/4 of the volume of the third pail. The barrel and all three pails hold integer numbers of liters. What is the smallest possible volume of the barrel?

Water fractions

If V is the volume of the barrel, then the volumes of the pails equal $2V/3$, $V/2$, and $4V/9$. The minimum positive integer V for which all these numbers are integers is 18. (N. Antonovich)

Morning meteors

Explain why we see more meteors from midnight to dawn than from evening to midnight.

Morning meteors

Meteorites hit the "morning" hemisphere of the Earth head-on, while those hitting the "evening" hemisphere are chasing after the Earth. So after midnight meteorites enter our atmosphere at a higher velocity. As they burn, they sparkle more brightly than before midnight. After midnight our eye will notice meteors of small cosmic particles that before midnight burn imperceptibly in the atmosphere. (V. Surdin)

Halving the pentagram

Prove that the area of the shaded portion of the star is exactly half the area of the whole star.

Halving the pentagram

The figure below shows that the painted and unpainted portions of the star can be cut into the same set of triangles. (N. Avilov)

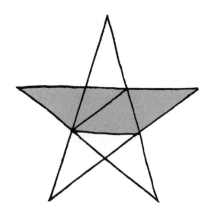

Vacuumed tubes

Air is pumped out of the tubes of some solar telescopes. Why is that?

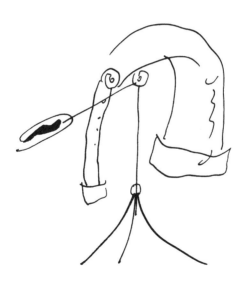

Vacuumed tubes

Air is pumped out to lessen turbulent thermal flows of air in the tube, which distort the image of the Sun. (V. Surdin)

English, Russian, and math

The accompanying number rebuses present two instances of long division (the same letters in each rebus correspond to the same digits, different letters correspond to different letters, and stars stand for any digit). One of the rebuses is in Russian (the words are ДЕСЯТЬ = TEN, ДВА = TWO, ПЯТЬ = FIVE) and written as they are in Russian schools (so we have 10 + 2 = 5). But you don't need to know Russian (or even English) to restore all the digits in the rebuses.

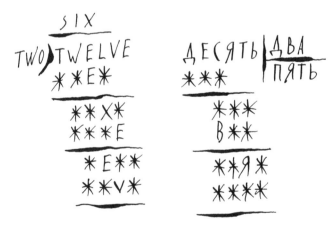

English, Russian, and math

Division "in English" is shown on the left; division "in Russian" is shown on the right. (E. Rekstins)

$$
\begin{array}{r}
986 \\
345\overline{)340170} \\
3105 \\
\hline
2967 \\
2760 \\
\hline
2070 \\
2070
\end{array}
$$

$$
\begin{array}{r|l}
385024 & 376 \\
376 & \overline{1024} \\
\hline
902 \\
752 \\
\hline
1504 \\
1504
\end{array}
$$

Crush on a map

The population of the United States is more than 200 million. It would seem that on a map with a scale of 1 : 5,000,000 (1 centimeter to 50 kilometers) there should be enough room for 1/5,000,000 as many people—that is, for more than 40. But you can check experimentally that five persons would have some difficulty squeezing onto such a map, and ten would find it impossible. Why?

Crush on a map

The area of a map with the scale 1 : k is $1/k^2$ that of the territory it represents. The number of people that can fit in a certain region is proportional to its area. So if this region is as big as the map in the problem, its "population" will be about $(2 \cdot 10^8)/(25 \cdot 10^{12}) = 0.000008$ person. (G. Galperin)

0.5 person

0.25 person

0.000008 person

0 person

Divisibility test

Prove that a number is divisible by 13 if and only if, after deleting its last digit and adding 4 times this last digit to the remainder, we get a number divisible by 13.

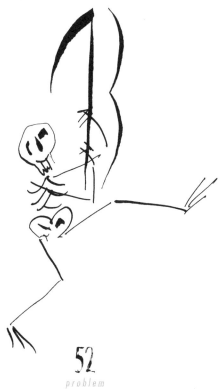

Divisibility test

Let the given number be $n = 10a + b$ (b is the last digit). Then the described operation yields $m = a + 4b$. Since $4n - m = 39a$ is a multiple of 13, the divisibility by 13 of the number m is equivalent to that of the number $4n$ and, therefore, of n. (B. Goncharenko)

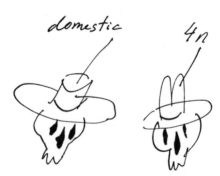

domestic

$4n$

Twilight in the mountains

Mountaineers say that high up in the mountains, twilight is noticeably shorter than down on the plains. What, in your opinion, is the reason for this?

Twilight in the mountains

Twilight is the period of semidarkness between sunset and nightfall. The daylight at this time of day is the result of sunlight being dispersed by the atmosphere at high altitudes, where the Sun has not yet set behind the horizon. High up in the mountains, the atmospheric layer over the Earth is thinner and the period of its illumination after sunset is shorter. So twilight in the mountains is shorter, too. (Planets devoid of atmosphere have no twilight at all, nor does the Moon.) (A. Buzdin)

Pythagoras revisited

The figure below shows a right triangle with three squares on its sides. The vertices of the squares are joined to form three triangles. Prove that these triangles have equal areas.

Pythagoras revisited

In the notation of the figure below, the area of triangle 1 is equal to $\frac{1}{2}ac \sin(180° - \alpha) = \frac{1}{2}ac \sin \alpha$, which is the area of the shaded triangle. Similarly, one can show that the other two triangles are also equal in area to the shaded one. (Actually, triangle 3 is even congruent to it.) (N. Avilov, V. Dubrovsky)

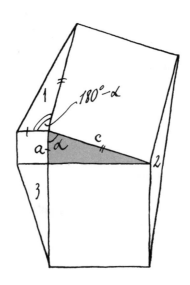

From points to players

Two precocious students from an elementary school took part in a chess championship at a nearby university. Each participant plays each of the others once. A win is worth one point, a draw is worth half a point, and players receive no points for a loss. The combined score of the elementary school students was 6.5; the scores of the university students all happened to be the same. How many university students participated in the championship?

From points to players

If x is the unknown number of university students, then each of $x + 2$ participants in the championship played $x + 1$ games, so their total score, equal to the total number of games, is $(x + 2)(x + 1)/2$. The total score of the x university students equals $(x + 2)(x + 1)/2 - 6.5 = \frac{1}{2}(x^2 + 3x - 11)$ and is equally distributed among them: each of them got $\frac{1}{2}(x + 3 - 11/x)$ points. This must be an integer number of half points, so 11 is divisible by x. It follows that $x = 11$ (in the case of $x = 1$, the score of each university student would be negative). (A. Markosian)

Square anniversary

In the year x^2 my nephew will be x years of age. In what year was he born?

Square anniversary

The nephew was born in the year $x^2 - x$. So $x^2 - x < 1996 \leq x^2$. A quick trial-and-error shows that $x = 45$ and the birth year is 1980. (L. Kurliandchik)

In search of consensus

Is there a temperature expressed by the same number of degrees in both the Celsius and Fahrenheit scales? (We remind you that these two uniform scales can be defined by the melting point of ice, which is 0°C or 32°F, and the boiling point of water, which is 100°C or 212°F.)

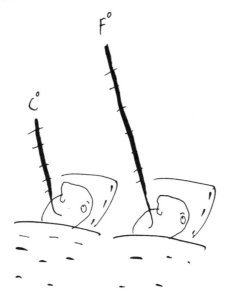

In search of consensus

The temperature t_F in Fahrenheit is a linear function of the temperature t_C in Celsius: $t_F = at_C + b$. The coefficients a and b can be found by equating the temperatures of the freezing point and boiling point: $t_F = (9/5)t_C + 32$. The equation $t_F = t_C$ yields $-40°F = -40°C$. (A. Savin)

Dirty windshield

Sometimes a car's windshield gets dirty when blobs of muddy water are tossed up by other vehicles, reducing visibility. Yet the experienced driver doesn't turn on the windshield wipers right away and avoids getting the glass wet for as long as possible. Why?

Dirty windshield

At first the small drops of dirty water hitting the windshield don't spread over it because the dry glass isn't wet enough. The windshield wipers moisten all the glass they touch, and the drops of dirty water hitting the wet glass spread due to capillary action. Because of the drastic reduction in visibility, experienced drivers hold off turning on the wipers. (S. Krotov)

Cheap remake

The figure below shows two flags measuring 9 × 12. Cut the flag on the left into four pieces so that you could stitch them together to make the flag on the right.

Cheap remake

See the figure below. (A. Shvetsov)

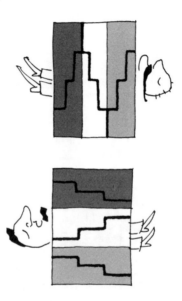

60

Greed punished

Koshchei the Immortal, a greedy and malicious tsar-sorcerer (and an indispensable character in Russian fairy tales), buried his ill-gotten treasure in a hole 1 meter deep. That didn't seem safe enough for him, so he dug his treasure up, deepened the hole to 2 meters, and buried his hoard again. He was still worried, so he dug up his hoard, made the hole 3 meters deep, and hid his treasure once more. But he just couldn't stop—he kept increasing the depth of the hole, to 4 m, 5 m, 6 m, and so on, each time extracting his property and burying it again, until on the 1,001st day he died of exhaustion. It's known that Koshchei digs a hole n meters deep in n^2 days. How deep was his treasure when he dropped dead? (Neglect the time needed to refill the hole each time.)

Greed punished

When Koshchei died, he left the treasure on the surface.

The first hole was dug in one day, the second in $2^2 = 4$ days, the third in $3^2 = 9$ days, and so on. So in $1 + 2^2 + 3^2 + ... + 13^2 = 819$ days, Koshchei buried his hoard at a depth of 13 m. Then he dug it up ($819 + 13^2 = 988 < 1,001$), but died before he could bury it 14 m down, because $819 + 14^2 = 1,015 > 1,001$. (D. Fuchs)

61

Zoo at home

Mademoiselle Dubois loves pets. All her pets but two are dogs, all but two are cats, and all but two are parrots. Those that are not dogs, cats, or parrots are cockroaches. She has more than two pets. How many pets of each kind does she own?

Zoo at home

Mlle Dubois has one dog, one cat, one parrot, and no cockroaches. (A. Rudin-skaya)

62

To make a parallelogram

A convex quadrilateral is cut along a diagonal, a congruent quadrilateral is cut along the other diagonal. Put the four pieces together to make a parallelogram.

To make a parallelogram

If *ABCD* is one of the given quad-
rilaterals, then translating triangle *ABD*
by vector *AC* into triangle CB_1D_1, we
get the required parallelogram
BB_1D_1D: its parts BB_1C and DD_1C are
congruent to the pieces $C'A'B'$ and
$C'A'D'$, respectively, of the second quadrilateral $A'B'C'D'$.
(V. Proizvolov)

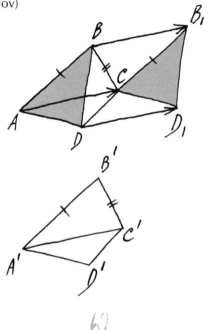

Cubes in water

You have two small cube-shaped plastic blocks of the same dimensions. The first block, floating in water, is submerged 2 cm; the second block is submerged only 1 cm. How deep will the lower block be submerged if the first block is placed on the second? What about the reverse (the second block is placed on the first)?

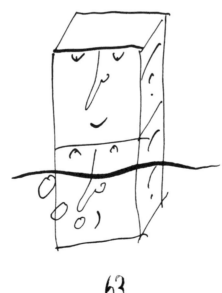

Cubes in water

The stacked blocks will be submerged
3 cm in both cases. (N. Dolbilin)

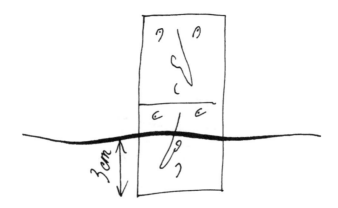

Monochromatic vertices

All the points of a circle are arbitrarily painted in two colors. Prove there is an isosceles triangle inscribed in the circle whose vertices are all the same color.

Monochromatic vertices

Consider an inscribed regular pentagon. At least three of its vertices are the same color (because there are only two colors). But any three of its vertices form an isosceles triangle. (I. Tonov)

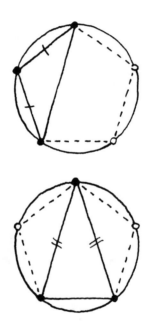

Squares in a row

Arrange the integers 1 through 15 in a row so that the sum of any two adjacent integers is a perfect square. How many ways can this be done?

solution

Squares in a row

The only perfect squares we can get by adding two integers between 1 and 15 are 4, 9, 16, and 25. If a, b, and c are three numbers in our row, then both $b + a$ and $b + c$ must be perfect squares, and a cannot equal c. A quick check shows that b cannot equal 8 or 9: for every other choice of b, there are two numbers in the required range that can be added to b to get a perfect square.

Therefore, the numbers 8 and 9 must be at either end of the row. This determines the order of the integers:

8 1 15 10 6 3 13 12 4 5 11 14 2 7 9

The only other way to get the required result is to read this solution backwards. (B. Recaman)

A feminist equation

Solve the number rebus SHE = (HE)², in which the same letters designate the same digits, different letters denote different digits.

A feminist equation

Let HE = x; then $x^2 - x$ is a three-digit number ending in two zeros—that is, it's divisible by 100. Since $x^2 - x = x(x - 1)$ is a product of two coprime numbers, one of them must be divisible by 25 and the other one by 4. If x or $x - 1$ equals $25k$, where $k \geq 2$, then the product $x(x - 1) \geq 50 \cdot 49$ and consists of more than three digits. So either $x - 1 = 25$ and $x = 26$ (which isn't divisible by 4), or $x = 25$ and $x - 1 = 24$, which yields the unique solution: $625 = 25^2$. (A. Savin, V. Dubrovsky)

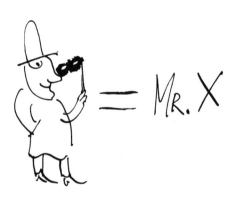

Making squares

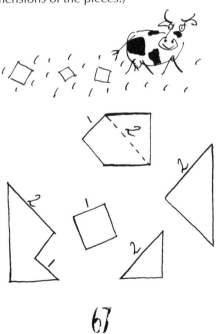

Take a piece of cardboard and cut out the polygons as shown. Then try to fit the pieces together to make a square (a) using each piece except the small square once, (b) using each of all five pieces once, (c) using each of the five pieces twice. (The numbers 1 and 2 in the figure denote the relative dimensions of the pieces.)

problem **67**

Making squares

See the figures below. (V. Dubrovsky)

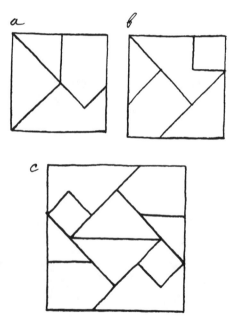

Musical thermos

When we fill a thermos with water, we hear a sound. How will its tone change while the thermos is being filled?

Musical thermos

The cavity of the thermos can be considered a resonator that amplifies sound frequencies close to the natural frequencies of the cavity. When you fill the thermos, the noise produced by the liquid has a wide spectrum of frequencies, but only the frequencies close to the resonant frequencies are amplified and are therefore audible to us. While the thermos is being filled, the length of the cavity decreases and the wavelengths of the resonant frequencies become shorter as well. As a result, the pitch of the tone should get higher. (A. Buzdin, S. Krotov)

In search of special pairs

Find the smallest positive integer such that the sum of its digits and that of the subsequent integer are both divisible by 17.

In search of special pairs

If the last two digits of a number are not 99, then, in passing to the next higher number, we either increase the digit-sum by 1 or (if the last digit was 9) decrease it by 8. So at least one of two such "next numbers" can't be divisible by 17. When a number ending in 99 (but not 999) is increased by 1, the digit-sum decreases by $9 + 9 - 1 = 17$, which is just what we need. However, numbers ending in 999 (but not 9999), when increased by 1, decrease their digit-sum by 26, which is not divisible by 17. Therefore, we want the smallest number ending in 00 whose digit-sum is divisible by 17. This is 8,900; so the answer is $8,900 - 1 = 8,899$. (G. Galperin)

Coins on a checkerboard

A number of coins are placed on each square of a checkerboard such that the sums on every two squares having a common side differ by one cent. Given that the sum on one of the squares is 3 cents, and on another one 17 cents, find the total amount of money on both diagonals of the checkerboard.

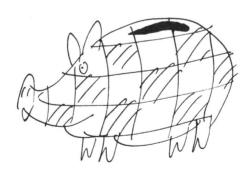

solution

Coins on a checkerboard

We can rotate the checkerboard so that the square *A* with the sum of 3 cents is located below and to the left of the square *B* with 17 cents. Let's move from *A* to *B* by making one-square steps up or to the right.

Since every step changes the sum in the current square by one and the numbers of right steps and up steps are both not greater than 7, the total increase of the sum is not greater than $7 + 7 = 14$. In fact, that's exactly what it is $(17 - 3)$. Therefore, squares *A* and *B* must be the bottom left and top right squares of the board, and whichever path we choose, each step must increase the sum by one; so after *any n* steps we find ourselves in a square with the sum of $3 + n$ cents. This uniquely determines the arrangement of sums. So the answer is $(3 + 5 + \ldots + 17) + (8 \cdot 10) = 160$. (V. Proizvolov)

B

10	11	12	13	14	15	16	17
9	10	11	12	13	14	15	16
8	9	10	11	12	13	14	15
7	8	9	10	11	12	13	14
6	7	8	9	10	11	12	13
5	6	7	8	9	10	11	12
4	5	6	7	8	9	10	11
3	4	5	6	7	8	9	10

A

Time machine

"You know," a friend of mine once said, "the day before yesterday I was 10 years old, and next year I'll be 13!" Can this be true?

Time machine

Yes, it can. My friend's birthday is on December 31, and our conversation took place on January 1. (S. Korshunov)

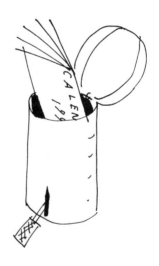

Mysterious pictographs

What's the rule for drawing the sequence of symbols as shown? Guess what figure should be drawn next.

Mysterious pictographs

If you cover the left half of each pictograph (which is the reflection of the right half—see below), you'll immediately recognize the sequence 1, 2, ..., 7 in a special kind of simplified writing. (Actually, this is the standard way the digits of a zip code must be written on an envelope in Russia so they can be read by a machine.) So the next figure in the line must be 8 plus its mirror image. (A. Zvonkin)

Rule:

Answer:

Disappearing pools

In karstic regions—that is, areas with irregular limestone formations, including caverns and underground streams—one can come upon unusual ponds. During the rainy season they gradually fill with water, but then they suddenly become surprisingly shallow. Why does that happen?

Disappearing pools

The unusual behavior of the water described in the problem can be explained by the siphon principle. The figure below is a schematic drawing of a karstic cavity that periodically empties the pool. Water fills the pool up to the level AA'; after that, the siphon is "switched on" and almost all the water leaves the pool. Pools where karstic cavities form siphons are called intermittent pools. (A. Buzdin)

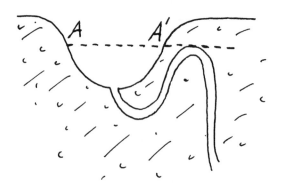

74

Calculating on the way

Alice used to walk to school every morning, and it took her 20 minutes from door to door. Once on her way she remembered she was going to show the latest issue of *Quantum* to her classmates but had forgotten it at home. She knew that if she continued walking to school at the same speed, she'd be there 8 minutes before the bell, and if she went back home for the magazine she'd arrive at school 10 minutes late. What fraction of the way to school had she walked at that moment in time?

Calculating on the way

The difference between the time it would take to go back home and then to school and the time to go straight to school is 10 + 8 = 18 minutes. The difference between the corresponding distances is simply twice the distance from the spot where Alice remembered about *Quantum* to her home. So this spot is 9 minutes away from home, which is 9/20 of the entire distance to school. (S. Dvoria-ninov)

Doublecross

Cut the two smaller crosses in the same way, each into four pieces, so that all eight pieces can be put together to form a similar cross with twice the area.

Doublecross

See the figure below. (L. Mochalov)

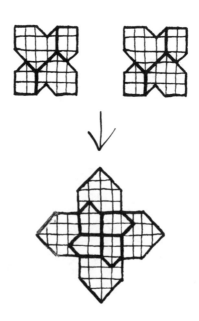

problem

76

Blond and blue-eyed

The proportion of blonds among blue-eyed persons is greater than among the population as a whole. Is it true that the proportion of blue-eyed people among blonds is greater than among the entire population?

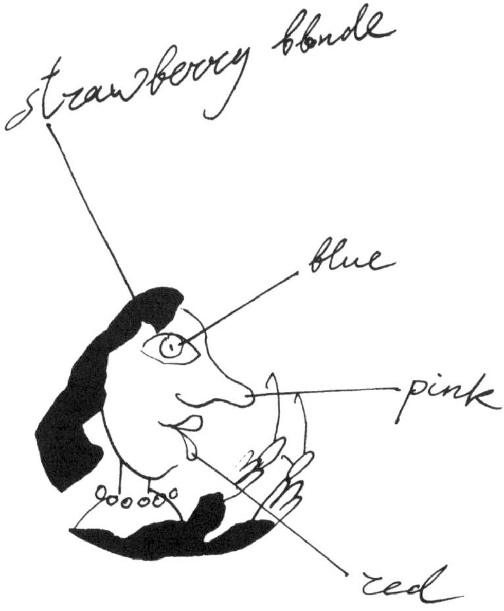
strawberry blonde
blue
pink
red

Blond and blue-eyed

Let a be the number of blond persons with blue eyes, b the number of all blonds, c the number of all blue-eyed people, and n the entire population. Then by the statement of the problem, $a/c > b/n$, or $an > bc$, or $a/b > c/n$. This means that the answer to the question is yes. (A. Savin)

77

Long heights

Does there exist a triangle, two of whose heights are not shorter than the sides on which they are dropped? If it does, what are its angles?

Long heights

The only kind of triangle that satisfies the condition is an isosceles right triangle. To prove this, consider a triangle ABC whose side $a = BC$ is not longer than the corresponding height h_a and $b = CA \leq h_b$. Obviously no height is longer than any of the sides drawn from the same vertex of a triangle. So we can write the following string of inequalities:

$$a \leq h_a \leq b \leq h_b \leq a,$$

which means that $a = b = h_a = h_b$. But the equality $a = h_b$ is possible if and only if a coincides with h_b—that is, a is perpendicular to b. (A. Savin)

78

Dripping hot and cold

Two identical laboratory pipettes are filled with water to the same level. The water is cold in one pipette and hot in the other. As the pipettes are emptied, the drops are counted. From which pipette will more drops fall?

cold   hot

Dripping hot and cold

A drop falls off the end of a pipette when the surface tension no longer counterbalances gravity. When the temperature of the water increases, the coefficient of surface tension and the force of surface tension decrease. The decrease is noticeable—about 20% when the temperature increases from 20°C to 100°C. Thus, the weight of each hot drop is less than that of a cold drop, and the number of hot drops is therefore greater.

There is another process that occurs during heating: the density of water decreases because of expansion. Generally speaking, this phenomenon plays a contrary role here. But the coefficient of thermal expansion for water is small, so this effect is much weaker than that due to surface tension and is practically absent in this problem. (A. Buzdin)

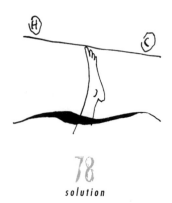

Two times two

Each letter in this "alphametic rebus" stands for some digit—different letters denote different digits, dots denote arbitrary digits. What number is TWO?

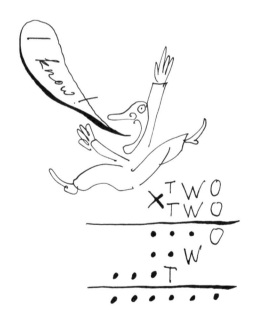

Two times two

TWO = 426. The last digit of the number in question, O, is such that O^2 ends in O. So it can be equal to 0, 1, 5, or 6. It's not zero, because the product TWO · O isn't zero (for a similar reason, W and T aren't zero either). It's not 1, because this product is a 4-digit number. It's not 5, because the products O · O, O · W, and O · T end in three different numbers. So O = 6. Now we know that 6 · W ends in W and 6 · T ends in T. An easy check shows that T and W can equal 2, 4, or 8. Since TWO · W and TWO · T are a 3-digit and a 4-digit number, respectively, the only possibility left is T = 4, W = 2. (A. Shvetsov)

Neat shearing

You have to make one square out of the three squares—2 × 2, 3 × 3, and 6 × 6—shown in the figure. How can you do this, cutting the squares into the smallest possible number of pieces?

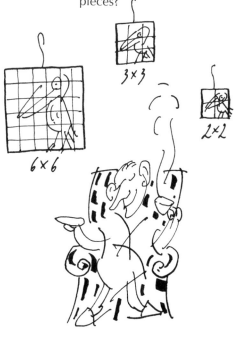

3 × 3

2 × 2

6 × 6

Neat shearing

See the figure below. (V. Proizvolov)

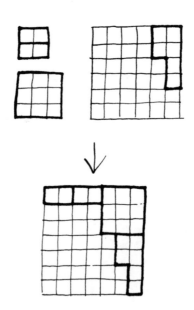

Equal sides, equal angles

In a quadrilateral *ABCD* the sum of the angles *ABD* and *BDC* is 180°, and the sides *AD* and *BC* are congruent. Prove that angles *A* and *C* of the quadrilateral are congruent.

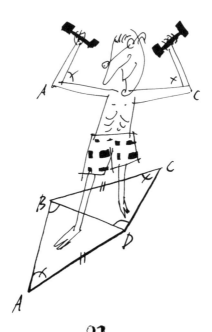

Equal sides, equal angles

Cut the quadrilateral along the diagonal *BD*, turn triangle *ABD* upside down, and put the piece back so that its vertices *B* and *D* change places. We get a triangle *A'BC*, because $\angle BDC + \angle BDA' = 180°$. This triangle is isosceles ($A'B = AD = BC$), so $\angle C = \angle A' = \angle A$. (V. Proizvolov)

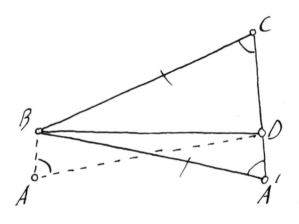

Retrochess

A chess knight traversed a 6 × 6 chessboard and returned to the starting square after visiting all the other squares once. Some of the squares still bear a trace of the knight's visit—the number of the square in the sequence of the knight's route. Restore the numbers of all the squares.

Retrochess

See the figure below. (A. Savin)

17	24	3	32	11	26
2	31	18	25	4	33
23	16	1	10	27	12
30	9	28	19	34	5
15	22	7	36	13	20
8	29	14	21	6	35

83

View of the Moon

In which case is the angular diameter of the Moon greater: when it's near its zenith or at the horizon?

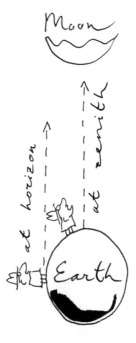

View of the Moon

It's clear from the figure that the Moon subtends a greater angle at the observer's position at its zenith than when it is on the horizon, so its angular diameter is greater in this position. (V. Surdin)

Calendar puzzle

Denoting different digits by different letters and the same digits by the same letters, I discovered that in the second half of a certain century *bd* there was a year *abcd*. What was that year?

bd B.C. or bd A.D.

Calendar puzzle

A quick search shows that there is no solution in Arabic numerals. (Here's why. Since *bd* is the number of a century, *b* is 1 or 2, but *b* ≠ 1, because *a* = 1. So *bd* = 20. Then, from the number of the year *abcd*, we get *b* = 9, which is a contradiction).

So our letters must stand for Roman numerals. A further search yields the following unique answer: *a* = M, *b* = X, *c* = C, *d* = I, so the year is MXCI (or 1091), and the century is XI (the 11th). (I. Akulich)

There are 12 persons in a room. Some of them always tell the truth, the others always lie. One of them said, "None of us is honest"; another said, "There is not more than one honest person here"; a third said, "There are not more than two honest persons here"; and so on, until the twelfth said, "There are not more than eleven honest persons here." How many honest persons are there in the room?

Worming out the truth

If there were k honest persons, the first k statements were wrong (and so were made by liars) and the last $12 - k$ statements were true (and so were made by honest persons). Therefore, $k = 12 - k$: there are $k = 6$ honest persons in the room. (D. Fomin)

Is it possible to inscribe ten different integers in the circles on the star shown so that the sum of the four numbers along each of the five lines is odd?

86 Odd sums on a star

No, it's impossible, because when the five odd sums are added up we must get an odd number; but on the other hand, each of the inscribed numbers enters this total sum twice, so it must be even. (A. Domashenko)

87

Mirror numbers

Two numbers are called mirror numbers if one is obtained from the other by reversing the order of digits—for example, 123 and 321. Find two mirror numbers whose product is 92,565.

Mirror numbers

The answer is 561 and 165. Clearly, the numbers in question must have three digits each. Let one of them be ABC = $(100 \cdot A) + (10 \cdot B) + C$ and the other CBA. Since $A \cdot C$ ends in 5, one of the numbers A and C—say, A—must be 5; and since $92,565 \div 500 < 200$, C = 1. To find B we notice that the 6 in the product is the last digit of $5 \cdot B + B = 6 \cdot B$, so B = 1 or B = 6. All that remains is to test the two possibilities. (A. Vasin, V. Dubrovsky)

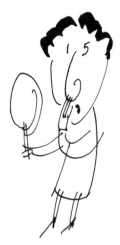

87
solution

The ends of a log are placed on two scales. The first scale shows 200 kg, the second only 100 kg. What is the log's mass? Where is its center of gravity?

Two scales, one log

The mass of the log is 300 kg. The distance between its center of gravity and the first scale is one half the distance between the center of gravity and the second scale. (V. Vigun)

Seen and unseen

One magazine lies on top of another one as shown. Is the part of the bottom magazine that we see bigger or smaller (in area) than the covered part?

Seen and unseen

The line *EF* makes it obvious that the area of the triangle *ABE* is exactly half that of the bottom rectangle *ABCD*. So the covered part of the rectangle has a greater area. By the way, this will remain true even if we replace the top rectangle with an arbitrary convex polygon that covers the vertices *A* and *B* and has a common point with the side *CD*. (A. Domashenko)

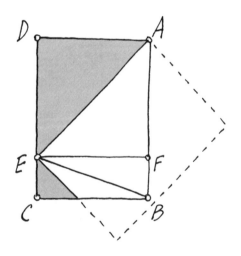

Clever tactics

Prince Ivan made up his mind to fight the three-headed, three-tailed dragon. So he obtained a magic sword that could, in one stroke, chop off either one head, two heads, one tail, or two tails. A witch revealed the dragon's secret to him: if one head is chopped off, a new head grows; in place of one tail, two new tails grow; in place of two tails, one new head grows; and if two heads are chopped off, nothing grows. What is the smallest number of strokes Prince Ivan needs to chop off all the dragon's heads and tails?

Clever tactics

The answer is nine. After Prince Ivan makes h_n ($n = 1, 2$) strokes that chop off n of the dragon's heads and t_k ($k = 1, 2$) strokes that chop off k tails, the numbers of heads and tails will be equal to $3 - 2h_2 + t_2$ and $3 + t_1 - 2t_2$, respectively. So we must find the solution to the equations

$$2h_2 - t_2 = 3,$$
$$2t_2 - t_1 = 3$$

with the least sum $h_2 + t_1 + t_2$ (of course, Ivan must choose $h_1 = 0$). It follows from the first equation that t_2 is odd; from the second equation we see that $t_2 \geq 3/2$, so $t_2 \geq 3$. Then $h_2 = (3 + t_2)/2 \geq 3$ and $t_1 = 2t_2 - 3 \geq 3$, so the total number of strokes is not less than 9. The numbers $h_2 = t_1 = t_2 = 3$ satisfy our equations, but we must make sure that it's really possible to inflict three strokes of each sort (so that, for instance, Ivan won't have to chop off two tails when there's only one tail left). One of the possible sequences is to chop off one tail (so that two new tails grow), then two tails (one new head grows), then two heads, and then repeat this series of strokes twice—after each of the three series the dragon loses one tail and one head. (V. Rusanov, V. Dubrovsky)

91

Dancing regularities

At a party each boy danced with three girls, and each girl danced with three boys. Prove that the number of boys at the party was equal to the number of girls.

Dancing regularities

Let N be the number of different pairs that danced at least once. Then the number of boys, as well as the number of girls, is equal to $N/3$. (V. Proizvolov)

Careless cashier

I went to the bank to cash a check. As the cashier gave me the money, I put it in my empty wallet without counting it. During the day I spent $6.23. When I checked my wallet in the evening, it contained exactly twice the amount of the check I had cashed. Strange! A little calculation revealed that while making the payment, the cashier had interchanged the figures for dollars and cents. What was the amount of the check?

Careless cashier

Your first try probably went something like this: the check was for x dollars and y cents; the cashier paid y dollars and x cents; since I was left with $2x$ dollars and $2y$ cents after spending \$6.23, the equations to determine x and y can be written

$$x - 23 = 2y,$$
$$y - 6 = 2x.$$

But the solutions to these equations are not positive integers, so another approach is needed. You have to consider the possibility that x is less than 23 so that, to subtract 23, you have to borrow 100 cents from the dollars figure. This will modify the equations as follows:

$$(x + 100) - 23 = 2y,$$
$$x + 77 = 2y,$$

and

$$(y - 1) - 6 = 2x,$$
$$y = 2x + 7.$$

The solution to this pair ($x = 21$, $y = 49$) has the right property. So the check was for \$21.49; the cashier paid \$49.21. I was left with \$42.98 (\$49.21 − 6.23), which is exactly double the amount of the check. (S. Sidhu)

Bubbles in a glass

An upside-down glass was immersed in a pan filled with hot water. After a while, air bubbles started coming out of the glass. Why?

Bubbles in a glass

The air in the glass was warmed by the hot water. It expanded, occupying more volume, so some air escaped around the rim of the glass.

Squares in a semicircle

Two squares are inscribed in a semi-circle as shown. Prove that the area of the big square is four times that of the small one.

Squares in a semicircle

It's obvious that in the figure, obtained by 90° rotation of the given big square about the circle's center, $OC = OA = AB/2 = CD/2$. So $AF = AE = AB/2$, and $AEDF$ is the given small square, whose side lengths are 1/2 those of the big one.

Strictly speaking, this argument is incomplete: we must prove that there is only one "small square" satisfying the requirements of the problem (then it will have to coincide with $AEDF$ in the figure). The uniqueness follows, for instance, from the fact that the vertex of the small square opposite A must lie at the intersection of the given circumference and the bisector of the angle EAF, which consists of a single point.

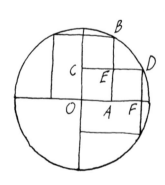

Rock to rock

From a pile of 1,001 rocks one rock is taken away and the rest of the pile is divided into two piles. Then one rock is taken away from a pile with more than one rock, and one of the piles is divided into two, and so on. Is it possible that after a number of such operations all piles have three rocks each?

Rock to rock

After every rearrangement of the rocks their number decreases by one, while the number of piles increases by one. So, if the number of operations was n, in the end we must have $n + 1$ piles of three rocks each and n rocks taken away. This means that the total number of rocks is $3(n + 1) + n = 4n + 3$. But the number 1,001 yields a remainder of 1, not 3, when divided by 4. So the answer to the question is no. (S. Rukshin, S. Genkin)

Logic behind coincidences

I've thought of a three-digit number such that each of the numbers 543, 142, and 562 coincides with it in exactly one decimal location. Guess what this number is.

Logic behind coincidences

If the first digit of the unknown number were 5, the second digit couldn't be 4 (from 543) and the third digit couldn't be 2 (from 562). So the first digit would have to be 1 (from 142). Similarly, the second digit isn't 4. Therefore, from 543, we see that the third digit is 3; then, from 142, that the first digit is 1; and, from 562, that the second is 6. This gives us the answer: 163. (V. Proizvolov)

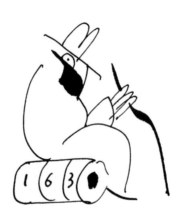

Entropy and Tesseract

While driving down an unfamiliar road, I noticed a sign that said: "Entropy—150 ents, Tesseract—110 tesses." Apparently the residents of Entropy measure distance in units called "ents," and the folks in Tesseract measure distance in "tesses." I drove further down the road. Before I came to either town, I saw another sign: "Entropy—10 ents, Tesseract—26 tesses." Find the point between Entropy and Tesseract where the distance from Entropy, measured in ents, equals the distance from Tesseract, measured in tesses.

Entropy and Tesseract

A little experimentation will show that I must be closer to Entropy than to Tesseract. Between the two signs I've driven 150 ents – 10 ents = 140 ents, and also 110 tesses – 26 tesses = 84 tesses. Equating these two, we find that 1 ent = 3/5 tess. It's not hard to find, then, that the distance from Entropy to Tesseract is 20 tesses. Suppose that at the point we seek I am x tesses from Tesseract and also x ents from Entropy. Then, measured in tesses,

$$x + \frac{3}{5}x = 20,$$

so $x = 12.5$ (tesses). This is the required position. (T. Stickels)

Tiling with dominoes

A chessboard is covered with 32 dominoes so that each domino covers exactly two squares. After counting the dominoes oriented horizontally and vertically, it was found that there are evenly many dominoes with each orientation. Will this be true for any covering of the chessboard with 32 dominoes?

Tiling with dominoes

Consider the 32 squares in the odd horizontal rows (the first, third, fifth, and seventh) of the chessboard. Each horizontal domino covers two or none of them, and each vertical domino covers exactly one of these squares. So the horizontal dominoes cover an even number n of these squares, and therefore the number of the remaining squares, $32 - n$, is also even. But it's equal to the number of vertical dominoes, which means that the answer to the question is yes. (V. Proizvolov)

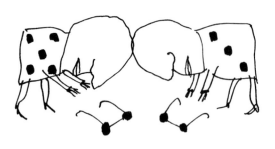

Halving it all

Three line segments are drawn in a convex quadrilateral: a diagonal and both midlines (the segments that join the midpoints of opposite sides). The other diagonal divides one of these segments in half. Prove that it bisects the other two segments as well.

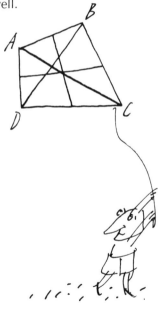

Halving it all

Suppose first that diagonal *AC* bisects *BD*. We will show that *AC* bisects midline *MN*. The key is to note that if *AC* bisects *BD*, then the (perpendicular) distances from *D* and *B* to line *AC* are equal. (This can be proved, for example, using congruent triangles.) This means that area(*ADC*) = area(*ABC*). Conversely, if area(*ADC*) = area(*ABC*), a similar argument shows that *AC* bisects *BD*. So *AC* bisects *BD* if and only if it divides the area of the quadrilateral in half.

We now show that this same condition is both necessary and sufficient for *AC* to bisect a midline. For suppose area(*ADC*) = area(*ABC*). Then, since area(*AMC*) = ½ area(*ABC*) and area(*ANC*) = ½area(*ADC*), we have area(*AMC*) = area(*ANC*), so *AC* bisects diagonal *MN* of quadrilateral *ANCM*.

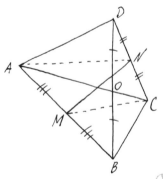

Another such argument shows that if *AC* bisects *MN*, then area(*ADC*) = area(*ABC*). So the conditions that *AC* bisects each of the three segments in the problem statement are all equivalent to the statement that *AC* bisects the area of the quadrilateral. (N. Netsvetayev, V. Dubrovsky)

100

Find a path to the center of the maze such that you get 100 by performing the operations along this path.

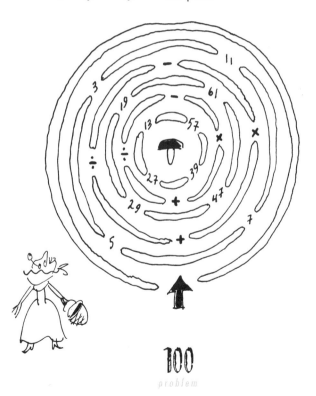

The path is $3 \cdot 29 + 13 = 100$.
(A. Larionov)